BOOK ANALYSIS

Written by Dominique Coutant-Defer
Translated by Jessica Foster

Around the World in Eighty Days

BY JULES VERNE

JULES VERNE   1

French novelist

AROUND THE WORLD IN EIGHTY DAYS   3

A wager followed through

SUMMARY   4

CHARACTER STUDY   11

Phileas Fogg

Passepartout

Fix

Mrs Aouda

ANALYSIS   13

Actantial model

Narrative outline

An adventure novel

FURTHER READING   19

JULES VERNE

- **Born in Nantes in 1828**
- **Died near Paris in 1905**
- **Notable works:**
    - *Journey to the Centre of the Earth* (1864), novel
    - *Around the World in Eighty Days* (1873), novel
    - *The Mysterious Island* (1874), novel

Born in Nantes in 1828, Jules Verne initially began studying law, then published a play and several short stories after 1852. He became friends with Jacques Argo (French author and explorer) and met explorers and scientists. His first novel, *Five Weeks in a Balloon* (1863), was incredibly successful. It was the beginning of the *Voyages extraordinaires*, which were composed of 18 short stories and 65 novels, including *Journey to the Centre of the Earth* (1864), *Twenty Thousand Leagues Under the Sea* (1869), *Around the World in Eighty Days* (1873), *The Mysterious Island* (1874) and *Michael Strogoff: The Courier of the Czar* (1876), among others. These works, which draw on a wealth of documents and combine adventure, anticipation and imagination, reflect the author's interest in the technological advances of his time and his passion for travelling.

In 1886, the death of his editor and friend Jules Hetzel, and the decline of his interest in science, marked a turning point in his career. He died in Amiens in 1905. Today, he is one of the most widely translated French language authors in the world.

AROUND THE WORLD IN EIGHTY DAYS

A WAGER FOLLOWED THROUGH

- **Genre:** adventure novel
- **Reference edition:** Vernes, J. (2012) *Around the World in Eighty Days*. Trans. Makepiece Towle, G. [Online]. Planet Publish. Available from: <http://www.planetebook.com/ebooks/Around-the-World-in-80-Days.pdf>
- **First edition:** 1873
- **Themes:** travel, adventure, challenge, discovery, chase, danger

Published in 1873, the adventure novel *Around the World in Eighty Days* was rapidly successful, and saw an exceptional print run, many translations, a theatre adaptation and the creation of related merchandise (small statues of Phileas Fogg, games, etc.). Readers are charmed by the incredible journey of the Englishman Phileas Fogg, who wagered that he could travel around the world in eighty days, using varied means of transport for this end: boat, train, elephant, sledge, etc. His journey would be emulated and several adventurers would really attempt to do the same, in the conditions given in the novel.

SUMMARY

CHAPTERS 1-3

The mysterious Phileas Fogg lives in London. He is a rich bachelor who spends most of his time at his club. One day in 1872, he hires a new valet: a Frenchman named Jean Passepartout who, having held several jobs, would like a peaceful job. He is happy to have found a job with Phileas Fogg, whose life runs like clockwork, and whose house is comfortable and tidy.

One evening, during a game of whist at the Reform Club, the men are talking about a significant theft committed at the Bank of England. But the thief will be caught quickly, as we can now get around the world in "[o]nly eighty days" (pp. 17-18), maintains Phileas Fogg, who wagers half his fortune on being able to complete the challenge and return on 21 December 1872. He explains the stages of the journey in detail.

CHAPTERS 4-5

On returning to his house, he orders Passepartout, who is not very happy, to pack a light suitcase, and informs him that he is going on an expedition and that he is taking half his fortune with him for the journey.

The English, who are interested in wagers and in geography, become very involved in the adventure and a new bond, the "Phileas Fogg bond", is listed on the stock exchange.

But soon, rumours fly that Fogg is the thief and that he is making this journey to escape from the police.

CHAPTERS 6-8

One week later, Fix, a detective who is posted in Suez, the first stop on Fogg's journey, is waiting for the traveller's arrival by boat, which he was warned of by London.

Phileas Fogg wants to 'visa' his passport (get a visa put inside) to mark his stop in Suez. However, Fix cannot arrest him, as he has not received an arrest warrant. The detective interrogates the loose-lipped Passepartout who informs him of his master's plan, in which the next stop is Bombay. He also mentions the large sum of money that Fogg is carrying. Fix decides to follow them.

CHAPTERS 9-11

On the boat, Fogg, who is unflappable, plays whist while Passepartout goes sightseeing at their ports of call. Thanks to favourable winds, the boat arrives in Bombay two days early. Fogg gets his passport 'visaed'. Fix is disappointed: the arrest warrant has still not arrived. Passepartout, meanwhile, has a shoe pulled off by a priest in a Hindu temple.

As the railway line that was meant to lead them to Calcutta is unfinished, Fogg decides to continue the journey on the back of an elephant, accompanied by Sir Cromarty, whom he met on the boat, and a guide.

CHAPTERS 12-15

During an uncomfortable journey through the forest, the Englishmen come across a Hindu funeral procession: a young widow must be burned with her husband's corpse. Fogg, who is still twelve hours ahead of schedule, decides to save her: when night falls, the group surrounds the pagoda where the sacrifice is set to take place and, having tricked the guards, Passepartout kidnaps the woman, who has already been tied to the stake.

After leaving Sir Cromarty, Fogg and Passepartout take a train to Calcutta, accompanied by the widow, whose name is Aouda. But Fix is on the scene and, to delay Fogg, has given Passepartout up to the local police for the incident with the shoes, on account of which he is sentenced to eight days in prison. Fogg decides to pay the hefty bail sum instead of wasting time.

CHAPTERS 16-19

On 25 October, they leave for Hong Kong and Fogg takes great care of Aouda. Fix climbs aboard discreetly, wholeheartedly wishing to arrest Fogg in Hong Kong, which is British territory. Passepartout, intrigued by the presence of Fix, who is once again alongside them, deduces that he is a member of the Reform Club who is ensuring that the journey goes as planned, while the detective thinks that the real reason for his presence has been discovered.

In Hong Kong, Fogg cannot find the relative that Aouda wanted to contact. The young woman therefore continues the journey with him and Passepartout.

In an opium den, Fix asks Passepartout to help keep Fogg (who will leave the following day for Japan) in Hong Kong, as the arrest warrant has still not arrived. He therefore reveals his real mission, but the valet is unwilling to believe in his master's dishonesty. Fix therefore has him smoke opium until he falls asleep, thus hoping to delay Fogg's departure.

CHAPTERS 20-23

The following day, Fogg learns that the boat, which was ready earlier than expected, left the day before, without anyone telling him. Fix is delighted that the next departure is not until eight days later, but Fogg finds a small boat that is leaving for Shanghai, and from there he can then reach Yokohama. He asks the police to find and repatriate Passepartout, who has not turned up. Fix also boards the boat.

The captain, motivated by the large reward promised to him by Fogg, does all he can to arrive in Shanghai on time, but a typhoon delays them. Nearing Shanghai, he puts his flag at half-mast to attract the attention of the liner that Fogg wants to take, but it is too late: it is already leaving the port.

Meanwhile Passepartout, awoken from his stupor and warned at the opium den of the early departure of the boat to Japan, boarded immediately that evening, believing his master to be aboard. On 13 November, he arrives in Yokohama, alone and without a penny to his name. To survive, he joins a troop of Japanese comedians and, during a performance, finds Fogg and Aouda again.

CHAPTERS 24-31

"On the ninth day after leaving Yokohama, Phileas Fogg had traversed exactly one half of the terrestrial globe" (p. 176). He is now en route to America. Fix is on the same boat as he is, with the famous warrant finally in hand. However, the warrant is unusable as Fogg is no longer in British territory. He therefore decides to follow him to London. On 3 December, they arrive in San Francisco.

After visiting the city and attending a lively political meeting, the travellers take the train to New York, the penultimate stop in the journey. Aouda seems to be getting increasingly attached to Fogg, who is merely showing her his usual courtesy.

During the journey through the United States, they admire the varied landscapes and Passepartout befriends a Mormon who explains the customs of his community. The passengers are horrified when, at top speed, the train crosses a bridge which looks as if it is about to give way under the snow and which collapses just after they have crossed it.

Fogg and his companions play whist to pass the time. An American who has already insulted Fogg during the meeting in San Francisco now accuses him of cheating. The two men decide to fight at the back of the train, but it is attacked by Sioux. As the driver is injured, Passepartout takes control of the operations and halts the train at the following station, which causes the Native Americans to flee.

Three passengers, including Passepartout, have disappeared. Fogg goes to find them, along with a few other men who were persuaded by the enormous reward promised to them by the Englishman. He manages to wrest them from the hands of the Native Americans, but he has lost twenty hours and the train has left without him.

Fix, who does not want to lose Fogg's trail, finds a sledge driver who can take them to Omaha (Nebraska), where they will board the train to Chicago. The journey is difficult due to the cold and wind, but they arrive in time. On 10 December, they are in Chicago, and on 11 December, New York. However, the boat which was supposed to take them to Liverpool left 45 minutes ago.

CHAPTERS 32-33

Fogg, by offering 8000 dollars to a boat captain, manages to board a boat to Bordeaux with his valet, Aouda and Fix (whose journey he pays for). Then he bribes the crew, locks up the captain and sets sail for Liverpool at top speed. As there is not much coal, part of the boat is burned to make the boilers work. "Phileas Fogg at last disembarked on the Liverpool quay, at twenty minutes before twelve, 21st December" (p. 258). Fix can now arrest him.

CHAPTERS 34-37

With his master in prison, Passepartout regrets not having warned him of Fix's mission, which might have allowed him to prepare his defence. But, several hours later, the detective repents and frees him: the real thief was arrested three days ago. Fogg therefore hires a private train, at an astronomical fee, to get to London, but he arrives five minutes too late.

He hides away in his house, almost ruined, as he has lost the bet, but he remains calm. Aouda confesses her love to him and asks him to marry her, which he accepts, and confesses his ardent feelings towards her too. Passepartout contacts a vicar and asks him to marry them the next day, a Monday. But the vicar says he cannot officiate at a wedding on a Sunday. The valet thus tells his master that he has arrived 24 hours early: as he was travelling east on his journey, Fogg was moving towards the sun and the days shortened by four minutes with every degree crossed. As the earth's circumference is 360 degrees, he has therefore gained a day in total and can triumphantly enter the Reform Club as he has won his bet.

CHARACTER STUDY

PHILEAS FOGG

At the age of 40, Phileas Fogg is introduced as a "polished man of the world" (p. 2), and as one of the most notable members of the Reform Club, where he spends most of his time. An enigmatic character, he intrigues people with his composure, his calmness and his quiet personality. He lives alone, and follows an unremitting routine. He does not think twice, however, before rising to the incredible challenge of getting around the world in eighty days, wagering half his fortune on it. None of the unexpected mishaps that come his way during the journey manage to rattle his British stoicism. He also manages to show courage, devotion and generosity, by saving Aouda from being burned at the stake and rescuing Passepartout from the Native Americans, for example, or by spending large amounts of money for them. The young widow has to confess her love for him first, so that he overcomes his hesitation.

PASSEPARTOUT

Passepartout is French: "he was an honest fellow, with a pleasant face, [...] with a good round head, such as one likes to see on the shoulders of a friend" (p. 9). Tired of the various jobs he has had (circus-rider, itinerant singer, sergeant fireman, etc.), he is looking for a calmer job when he goes to work for Fogg. However, he then ends up following him throughout his chaotic adventure, which he ends up getting a taste for, and in which his improvisation allows him to resolve some critical situations. He gradually becomes closer to his strange master and supports him during his ridiculous wager.

FIX

Fix is one of the detectives sent to the main British ports to arrest Fogg, who is suspected of theft. He is a "small, slight-built personage, with a nervous, intelligent face" (p. 32). As the arrest warrant he needs to intercept Fogg always arrives too early or too late in the various cities they travel to, he is forced to follow him and joins the adventurous journey in spite of himself. Deeply irritated by Fogg at the beginning of the story, he ends up having respect and admiration towards him.

MRS AOUDA

Condemned by Hindu custom to be burned alongside her husband's body, Mrs Aouda is saved by Fogg and his companions, who come across her in India. This young and beautiful Indian woman received an English education. To save her from being hunted, Phileas decides to take her with him. She is extremely grateful to Passepartout, who saved her from the flames, and quickly falls in love with Fogg who cares for her constantly. She ends up proposing to him.

ANALYSIS

ACTANTIAL MODEL

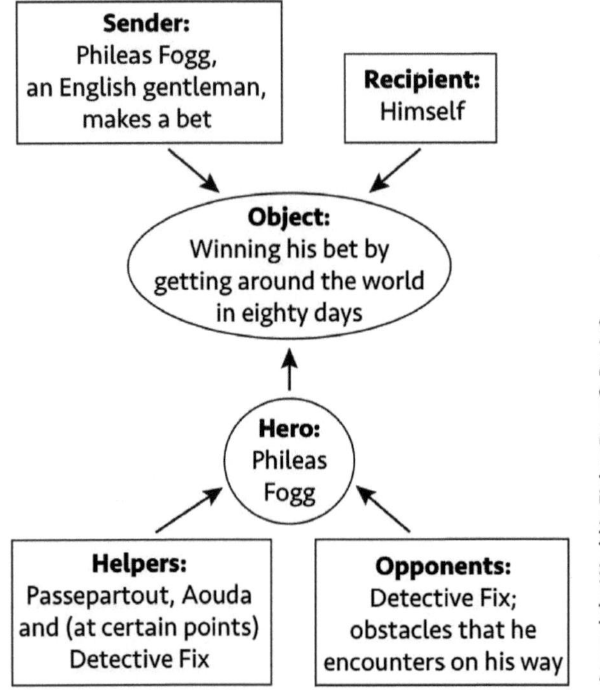

NARRATIVE OUTLINE

Initial situation: at the beginning of the story, when the scene is set and the characters are introduced, the situation is balanced, meaning that it has no reason to evolve.

- Phileas Fogg, an English gentleman of few words, leads an orderly life in London.

Disruptive element: an event that disrupts the situation and triggers the story itself.

- He wagers with the members of his club that he can travel around the world in eighty days.

Developments: these are events provoked by the disruptive element which lead to an action or actions on the part of the main character to resolve the problem.

- He sets off with Passepartout, his new valet. He travels through India (where he is joined by Aouda, a widow who was condemned to death), China, Japan and America. Several obstacles block his way and he is followed by the detective Fix, who believes he is guilty of a bank robbery. But he arrives in London five minutes too late, thus believing he has lost his bet. He accepts Aouda's marriage proposal.

Outcome: this puts an end to the developments and leads to the conclusion.

- He learns that he has in fact arrived a day early due to the time difference.

Conclusion: this is the end of the story. The situation is stable again, like the initial situation, but has undergone transformations.

- He returns to his club triumphant, as has won his wager.

AN ADVENTURE NOVEL

The literary genre of adventure novels, which *Around the World in Eighty Days* belongs to, came about during the second half of the 19th century, following novels such as Daniel Defoe's *Robinson Crusoe* (1719). These novels were mainly written in the United Kingdom, with authors such as Joseph Conrad (*Lord Jim*, 1900) and Robert Louis Stevenson (*Treasure Island*, 1883), and in France with Alexandre Dumas (*The Three Musketeers*, 1844; *The Count of Monte Cristo*, 1845) and Jules Verne. It was popular literature, often appearing as series in newspapers, and which above all aimed to provide entertainment and escapism for its readers.

Adventure novels generally have the following characteristics, which we also find in the work studied here:

- They portray many extraordinary developments. We can cite as examples the many obstacles that Phileas Fogg has to face: the missed trains or boats, Aouda's rescue, the attack of the Sioux, Passepartout's disappearance, etc.
- Suspense is constantly built up to keep the reader interested, thanks to several unexpected developments, which sometimes casts suspicion on how truthful the story is. The final development in *Around the World in Eighty Days* is a good example of this: while the saddened reader believes that Fogg has lost the bet, he learns in the

very final pages that a small time difference, accumulated throughout his journey, has actually made him gain a day.

- They make reference to an exotic reality. The many countries travelled through by the Englishman are described in detail by Jules Verne, as are the customs of the local people. Thus, the Hindu rites, the opium dens in China or even the American political meetings are depicted with realism.
- We encounter stock characters, often without much psychological depth. Phileas Fogg is characterised by his lucidity and his calmness in any situation, while Passepartout is a fearless, enthusiastic man who is completely devoted to his master. The beautiful Aouda, the only female character in the novel, is secretly in love with the mysterious Fogg.
- The world depicted is simplistic. There is a clear distinction between good and evil: Fogg, intelligent and generous, and Passepartout, resourceful and courageous, represent good; while Fix, the narrow-minded detective, the cruel Hindu priests and the savage Sioux, for example, embody evil.
- Finally, the target audience is young adults. The simplistic world of adventure novels perhaps explains the young age of most of the genre's readership: they are enticed by Phileas Fogg's bold initiative and can identify with Passepartout, for example, whose courage allows them to save Aouda from death or stop a train travelling at top speed.

Around the World in Eighty Days thus fits the definition of an adventure novel as given by Robert Louis Stevenson: "The reconstruction of every little boy's dream."

We want to hear from you!
Leave a comment on your online library
and share your favourite books on social media!

FURTHER READING

REFERENCE EDITION

- Vernes, J. (2012) *Around the World in Eighty Days*. Trans. Makepiece Towle, G. [Online]. Planet Publish. Available from: <http://www.planetebook.com/ebooks/Around-the-World-in-80-Days.pdf>

MORE FROM BRIGHTSUMMARIES.COM

- Reading guide – *Journey to the Center of the Earth* by Jules Verne
- Reading guide – *The Castle of the Carpathians* by Jules Verne
- Reading guide – *Twenty Thousand Leagues Under the Sea* by Jules Verne